NEW LIFE GUIDE

New Believer's Handbook for the Christian Faith.

RELEVANT PAGES PRESS

Published by Relevant Pages Press, Charleston, South Carolina.

Unless otherwise stated, scripture quotations are taken from the Holy Bible, New Living Translation (NLT), copyright © 1996, 2004. Used by permission of Tyndale House Publishers, Inc., Wheaton, Illinois 60189.

Other translations have also been used:
TLB – The Living Bible, Tyndale House Publications. All rights reserved.
NKJV – New King James Version, Thomas Nelson. All rights reserved.
NASB – New American Standard Bible, Foundation Publications. All rights reserved.

ISBN-10: 06-9264319-2
ISBN-13: 978-0692643198

Printed in the United States of America.

Contents:

The Basics

Jesus, who is He?

Jesus is revealed in the New Testament as the King of Kings. His miraculous birth, life, teachings, miracles, and triumph over death show his true identity. Jesus alone is the Son of God. In the Gospel of Mark, Jesus demonstrates his divinity by healing diseases, casting out demons and overcoming death. Although he had the power to become the king of the earth, Jesus chose to live as the perfect example of a human, by obeying God the Father, and dying for us. Jesus provided the perfect sacrifice for our sin so we could be saved. However, he is also fully God and therefore able to reveal God to us clearly and accurately.

Did He really exist?

Some people may question his existence. Evidence from other sources outside the New Testament includes Roman historians (Tacitus and Suetonius) and a Jewish historian (Josephus). There are also original ancient copies of manuscripts which mention Jesus, that date back to New Testament times written in both Greek and Hebrew.

What did He say?

Jesus made many claims about himself and these have been recorded in the Bible.
He claimed to be:

- The Son of God - *"Anyone who has seen Me has seen the Father"* (John 14:9)
- The only way to God the Father - *"Jesus answered, I am the way the truth and life. No one comes to the Father except through Me"* (John 14:6)
- Victorious over death, giving us never ending life - *"I am the resurrection and the life. Those who believe in me, even though they die like everyone else, will live again"* (John 11:25-26)

Is Jesus a prophet, a good man, or the Son of God?
Matthew 16:13-17

Where's the evidence?

There is evidence to support what Jesus claimed. He taught hundreds of people on occasions such as the Sermon on the Mount (Matthew Chapters 5, 6, & 7).

He performed many miracles - like healing people of diseases (Luke 5:12-13). He fulfilled Old Testament prophecy, and conquered death by being raised from the dead.

The immediate effect of Jesus' life was the birth and development of the church. Christians were persecuted as a result. A sobering fact remains, each one of his disciples died a cruel death as a consequence of declaring Jesus to be the Son of God. They would not have given their lives for someone who did not exist.

"A man who was merely a man and said the sort of things Jesus said would not be a great moral teacher, he would either be a lunatic - on a level with a man who says he is a poached egg - or else he would be the Devil of Hell. You must make your choice. Either this man was and is the Son of God or else a madman or something worse…but do not let us come up with any patronizing nonsense about His being a great human teacher. He has not left that open to us, he did not intend to." - C.S. Lewis

Recommended reading:

Mere Christianity
C.S. Lewis, HarperOne

More than a Carpenter
Josh McDowall, Tyndale Momentum

Good News

A Big Decision

You need to do several things to receive Christ: *ADMIT* your spiritual need as one who sins; *REPENT* and be ready to turn from your sin; *BELIEVE* that Jesus died for you; and *RECEIVE* through prayer, Jesus into your life.

Pray something like this from your heart:

Dear Lord Jesus,
I know that I am a sinner and need Your forgiveness. I believe that You died for my sins. I want to turn from my sins. I now invite You to come into my heart and life. I want to trust and follow You as my personal Lord and Savior. Thank you for saving me. Amen.

Congratulations! You have just made the most significant decision of your life based on this truth: *"That if you confess with your mouth Jesus is Lord and believe in your heart that God raised him from the dead, you will be saved"* (Romans 10:9 NLT).

People's experiences of receiving Christ are different. Some know instantly that they are changed, for others it is a more   gradual process. *"When someone becomes a Christian he becomes a brand new person inside. He is not the same anymore. A new life has begun"* (2

Did you know there is rejoicing in the presence of the angels over you?
Luke 15:8-10

Corinthians 5:17 LB).

The Benefits Start Now

You have received forgiveness of your sins and assurance of eternal life, through faith in God's only son, Jesus. *"I write this to you who believe in the Son of God, so that you may know you have eternal life."* (1 John 5:13). You are not condemned, for the power of

God has freed you through Jesus from the hold of sin that leads to death (Romans 8:1-2).

God has now adopted you into His family, *"For all who are led by the Spirit of God are children of God. You should not be like fearful cowering slaves. You should behave instead like God's very own children, adopted into His family – calling Him father, dear father. For His Holy Spirit speaks to us deep in our hearts and tells us that we are God's children. And since we are His children, we will share His treasures – for everything God gives to His Son, Christ, is ours, too. But if we are to share in His glory, we must also share in His suffering"* (Romans 8:14-17).

Like a good earthly father who buys tailor-made presents for each of his children, so it is with our heavenly Father – he has wonderful gifts for all his children. As each family member is special, so he has designated specific gifts for each of us. There are different kinds of spiritual gifts, but it the same Holy Spirit who is the source of them all. God works in our lives in different ways, but it is the same God who does the activity. These gifts are a means of us helping the entire church (1 Corinthians 12:1-11).

Personal God

You can know God personally - as presumptuous as that may sound. God loves you and He created you to get to know him for yourself. God is so eager to establish a personal, loving relationship with you, that he has made all the arrangements necessary. *"And this is the way to have eternal life – to know you, the only true*

God, and Jesus Christ, the one you sent to earth" (John 17:3). He has been patiently waiting for you to respond to his invitation.

Sin separates us from God, so Jesus gave his life as a sacrifice to take the sin of the world and enable us to have a personal relationship with him. When we receive his invitation we can then establish an ongoing individual connection with God the father. You don't have to do a single thing to make him love you more, as his love is unconditional.

How do we get to know our adoptive father better?
Ephesians 1:17-18 & Romans 8:26

Almighty God

God is mighty and powerful, let's face it, He created us! For that reason, we should treat Him with the reverence that He deserves. Mary, the mother of Jesus said, *"I am the Lord's servant and I am willing to accept whatever he wants"* (Luke 1:38). Our attitude should be the same.

God has a wonderful plan for our lives and He wants us to follow it so we will be successful in all that we do. *"For I know the plans I have for you, says the Lord. They are plans for good and not for disaster, to give you a*

11

future and a hope" (Jeremiah 29:11). Therefore, we need to   consult God before making major decisions (Isaiah 30:1-2). God promises to direct us in all that we do (Psalm 32:8; John 10:3-4).

God guides us when we read the Bible (Psalm 119:105). He also guides us by speaking to us in a small voice which requires concentration to hear (1 Kings 19:11). This is often recognized through a good thought, a strong impression or a feeling. Nevertheless, it can be tested, if it is God, it will be loving, encouraging and full of the peace of God (Acts 13:1-3).

---

*God loves us so much
He died to prove it.*
Isaiah 53:6 &
2 Corinthians 5:21

Throughout the Bible the Holy Spirit has guided people - sometimes by unusual means - take a look at the following examples. Angels announced the birth of Jesus (Luke 8-11); Samuel heard an audible voice when he was called to be a prophet (1 Samuel 3:4-14); and the apostle Paul was told to go on a missionary journey by seeing a vision (Acts 16:9-10). The Holy Spirit gives direction to those who ask, yet He may not use such elaborate methods as these to get your   attention.

We are expected to use our minds to think things through, and to listen to good advice (Proverbs

12

12:15).　　　　　　　Nevertheless, we are ultimately responsible to God for our actions. Sometimes God opens doors for us and　　　sometimes He closes them.

Recommended reading:

The Father Heart of God
Josh McDowell, Harvest House Publishers.

Unlimiting God
Richard Blackaby, Multnomah Books.

A New Beginning

Transformation

When we become a Christian (a follower of Jesus Christ), or are 'born again,' there is a transformation that takes place within us. God's Holy Spirit comes to live within us (Romans 8:9). Our experiences vary, some immediately know the difference, and for others it is more gradual. *"But to all who believed him and accepted him, he gave the right to become children of God"* (John1:12). He transforms our characters and relationships from the inside.

Check some of the following alterations which have begun in your life:
- ∂ A new passion for God
- ∂ A hunger to read the Bible
- ∂ A desire to worship God
- ∂ A knowledge of forgiveness
- ∂ A new concern for others
- ∂ An enjoyment of meeting with other Christians

The Bible says, *"For God so loved the world that He gave his only Son, so that everyone who believes in Him will not perish but have eternal life"* (John 3:16). God loves us so much that he wants us to encounter his reconciliation and life.

Being at peace with God is not automatic, due to our nature we are separated from God, through sin. *"For all have sinned, all fall short of God's glorious standard"* (Romans 3:23). Man has tried to bridge this separation in lots of ways: through philosophy, good works, religion, and morality, to name a few. However, none of them reach His perfect standard. The penalty for sin is death, *"For the wages of sin is death, but the free gift of God is eternal life through Christ Jesus our Lord"* (Romans 6:23).

What does it mean to be born again?
John 3:1-8, 16

If someone commits a crime, do we incriminate the judge for being unreasonable when the sentence is announced and the man is condemned? Of course not! The criminal was personally responsible for his destiny. In the same way we are responsible for the sin we commit. Yet we try to disguise sin with so many things that may 'earn' our reconciliation to God.

The good news is that the gap of separation between us and God was bridged through his unconditional love. God substituted his son for us, *"For the Son of man (Jesus) has come to save that which was lost"* (Matthew 18:11 NKJV). Jesus gave up his life to be crucified, and rose from death three days later in order to take the punishment for our wrong-doings (1 Peter 2:24).

15

New Life

Jesus' love for us is brilliant news because it delivers new life.   His message is for all people in every nation. Because Jesus is God's Son, we can completely trust what He says, by accepting Him we can have a new life that lasts forever. When Jesus rose from the dead, He proved that He was God; that He could   forgive sin; and that he has the power to change our lives. The resurrection shows Jesus' all-powerful life for us – not even death could stop his plan of offering us eternal life. By trusting in Jesus for   forgiveness, we can begin a new life with Him.

To obtain this new life we have to leave our sinful habits behind. *"What this means is that those who become Christians become new persons. They are not the same anymore, for the old life is gone. A new life has begun!"* (2 Corinthians 5:17). As new Christians we should not live like unbelievers, but follow Jesus' role model. *"Don't copy the behavior and customs of this world, but let God transform you into a new person by changing the way you think. Then you will know what God wants you to do, and you will know how good and pleasing and perfect his will really is"* (Romans 12:2).

Why not take a moment to give Jesus the right to be Lord of your life? You may like to use this prayer, *"Jesus, I give myself to you in complete surrender, please give me the determination to follow you."* Those who become Christians without this total submission to God, do not grow into maturity, they instead become like babies - as the Bible refers to them in Hebrews 5:12-14.

Water Baptism

Water baptism is an outward sign of your new commitment to following Jesus. According to Jesus water baptism is an essential part of following him. It is a strong way for us to proclaim God's power in our lives. The apostle Paul wrote, *"...when we became Christians and were baptized with Christ Jesus, we died with him. For we died and were buried with Christ by baptism. And just as Christ was raised from the dead by the glorious power of the Father, now we also may live new lives"* (Romans 6:3-4).

Water baptism symbolizes dying to our old sinful nature, then being raised by Jesus, washed clean on the inside. It is a public testimony of our commitment to Christ and our desire to follow him.

Should we wait to take the plunge?
Acts 2:41 &
Acts 8:35-38

Jesus told his disciples, before he returned to heaven, *"Go into all the world and preach the Good News to everyone, everywhere. Anyone who believes and is baptized will be saved. But anyone who refuses to believe will be condemned"* (Mark 16:15-16). These words are significant as they were his last spoken to the disciples.

17

Perhaps you have been baptized as an infant. Or maybe your last church did not practice believer's baptism. It is an important public declaration of your faith and your firm commitment to follow Jesus. Infants cannot do that. Since you have invited Jesus to be your Lord, water baptism is your next step.

The Holy Spirit's Power

The only effective way to live the Christian life and be a witness for Jesus is by the power of the Holy Spirit. We need his help to change our lives and make us more Christ-like. It is very difficult to be an effective Christian without his help. The apostle Paul wrote about some of the benefits of living a Spirit filled life, *"But the fruit of the Spirit is love, joy, peace, patience, kindness, goodness, faithfulness, gentleness and self-control. Against such things there is no law. Those who belong to Christ Jesus have crucified the sinful nature with its passions and desires. Since we live by the Spirit, let us keep in step with the Spirit"* (Galatians 5:23-25).

For a long time the person and work of the Holy Spirit has been ignored, reasoned out, or opposed by some churches. The Holy Spirit cannot be ignored, he is part of the trinity (tri = 3): God the Father, God the Son (Jesus), and God the Holy Spirit. This may be a difficult concept to grasp, let's use an illustration to clarify things: water can be represented as ice, steam or liquid – yet it is the same substance - water. It is also true to say that God can be represented in three different ways: as the Father, the Son and the Holy Spirit, the three are one God.

Now we realize who the Holy Spirit is, we need to understand that he is important to our lives. Before Jesus left his disciples to return to heaven he said, *"I will ask the Father, and He will give you another Helper, that He may be with you forever"* (John 14:16 NASB). Jesus wants you to live your life with the power of the Holy Spirit every day. He told his disciples who lacked the power to tell others about Christ, *"But when the Holy Spirit has come upon you, you will receive power (dynamite) and will tell people about me everywhere"* (Acts 1:8). At our invitation, the Holy Spirit can enable us to lead dynamic, fulfilling and abundant new lives. Why not ask the Holy Spirit to do just that?

Why is it important to invite the Holy Spirit to come upon us?
Acts 1:8, Romans 8 &
Acts 2:4

Throughout the Bible the Holy Spirit's work is evident. In Genesis (the first book of the Bible), the Holy Spirit brought order out of chaos throughout the creation of the universe (Genesis 1:20), and gave life to man (Genesis 2:7). The Old Testament records the Holy Spirit coming upon various individuals to give them strength for particular tasks. Take for example, Deborah who needed leadership skills (Judges 4, 5) and Samson who required strength (Judges 15:14-15).

19

In the Old Testament the prophets (individuals who God gave special messages) spoke of a new thing, that the Holy Spirit would be poured on all people (Joel 2:28-29). But this and other prophecies remained unfulfilled for several hundred years. Later, the New Testament documents much activity of the Holy Spirit, with the coming of Jesus (Luke 1 & 2). John the Baptist - who prepared the way for Jesus' arrival - baptized (immersed) with water. He spoke of one who is greater than himself (Jesus) who would baptize with the Holy Spirit. Jesus received power through the filling of the Holy Spirit at his baptism (Luke 3:21-22).

Towards the end of Jesus' life he predicted that the Holy Spirit's power would be given to all those who believed in him (Luke 24:49). The Holy Spirit would act as a comforter to the disciples, who would soon lose Jesus from this earth. The Holy Spirit was given to empower them for their work (Luke 1:4-5, 8). It is through the Holy Spirit that we are equipped to do God's will, without him we can only work at our own level and strength.

Recommended reading:

Know What You Believe, Paul E. Little,
IVP Books, ISBN 0830834230

Questions of Life, Nicky Gumbel,
Alpha   Books,   ISBN   1934564664

Spiritual Growth

The Bible

Despite the Bible being the world's number one best seller, many Christians do not read it regularly. This is often   because they cannot find a correlation between the ageless principles of God's Word and today's problems.   Therefore, it is helpful to read a new translation which is easy to use - like the *New International Version*, for example.

Applying God's Word is a vital part of our relationship with God, it is the evidence that we are obeying him. *"And remember, it is a message to obey, not just to listen to. If you don't obey, you are only fooling yourself"* (James 1:22). The Bible is God's Word to us, his spoken revelation.

The Bible is our influence for teaching, improving, equipping and correcting us for God's service. It is like spiritual food, it keeps us strong as a Christian. *"Yet faith comes from listening to this message of good news – the Good News about Christ"* (Romans 10:17). It is good to read through the Bible taking a book at a time,   before going on to something new. If you are looking at the Bible for the first time, you might want to start with the Gospel of

John, found in the New Testament. It deals with questions related to your new life.

The Bible also speaks to those who are not Christians about the love of God, personified through Jesus. *"But these are written so that you may believe that Jesus is the Messiah, the Son of God, and that by believing in him you will have life"* (John 20:31).

> *Christians believe that the Bible is the most treasured and powerful book ever written.*
> 2 Timothy 3:15-17

Getting the most from God's Word, and learning how he speaks through it is important. Firstly, develop a regular pattern of   reading and plan ahead to make it a routine (remember, it takes 30 days to form a habit). Secondly, choose a quiet place to be alone with God – this may take creativity - especially if there are small children in the home! Lastly, the following procedure may be helpful:

- ∂ Ask God to speak to you
- ∂ Read a Bible passage (You may want to start reading through the Gospel of John)
- ∂ Ask yourself questions (What does it mean? Can I apply it to my situation?)
- ∂ Respond in prayer
- ∂ Apply it to your life by putting it into practice

Prayer

Prayer is talking and listening to God. It should be one of the most important activities we do every day. It is significant that the whole trinity is involved. Jesus taught His disciples to pray, *"Our Father in heaven, may your name be honored"* (Matthew 6:9). We pray through the Son, *"Now all of us, both Jews and Gentiles, may come to the Father through the same Holy Spirit because of what Christ has done for us"* (Ephesians 2:18). This is accomplished in the Spirit, *"And the Holy Spirit helps us in our distress. For we don't even know what we should pray for, nor how we should pray. But the Holy Spirit prays for us with groanings that cannot be expressed in words"* (Romans 8:26).

God loves to hear us pray. We can pray anytime we want to – on our knees; driving our car; at home; in the church – it doesn't matter where we are. Prayer is the vehicle that enables us to develop a relationship with God. By doing so, we are following Jesus' example, by spending time in God's presence. The Bible suggests that it is good to pray: *always* (1 Thessalonians 5:17); *alone* (Matthew 6:6); and *with others* (Matthew 18:19). It is excellent to form a habit of praying daily, this will help develop our relationship with God.

How should we pray?
Matthew 6:9-13

There are some wonderful benefits to praying. The Bible points out that God will give us good gifts when we ask for them in prayer (Matthew 7:7-11). The Bible clearly states, *"But, when you pray, go away by yourself, shut the door behind you, and pray to your heavenly Father secretly. Then your Father, who knows all secrets, will reward you"* (Matthew 6:6). Not only will we receive rewards from God, but we are also guaranteed joy (John 16:24) and peace (Philippians 4:6-7). We can only benefit through prayer.

God doesn't always answer our prayers the way we think he should. We can use an illustration of a traffic light to understand this better. When we drive down the road sometimes the light is green which enables us to go safely on our way. At other times the light may be yellow, which indicates that we must wait for it to change - although, we could ignore it and plough straight ahead, however, it would not be beneficial to us and may even be dangerous. Lastly, the light is sometimes red, this forces us to stop and delay our trip. We all get frustrated at times and often don't understand the logic of this. Albeit, if we drove on ahead we would unquestionably be in jeopardy, and would almost certainly get stopped by the police further along our   journey.

God speaks to us through prayer and the answer may be: *yes, no, or wait.* Although we don't always understand His will for our lives at the time, further down life's road, we can often see more clearly the reason for his guidance and decision. If we check our hearts we may find several reasons why God is unable to give us what we're asking for: our motives may be wrong; we could be harboring unconfessed sin; and sometimes we hold on to unforgiveness.

Small Groups

Read Luke 8:4-15. Here Jesus told a story about a farmer who went out to sow some seed. This story was used to illustrate a point he was making about God's Word. Some seed fell along the path and never got planted at all; some fell on rocky ground, at first it sprang up but didn't put roots down; some fell among thorns and was choked; other seed fell on good ground. Your commitment to Jesus is reflected in one of these ways, therefore be determined to be a fruitful seed, growing up as a strong believer.

One of the ways in becoming a strong believer is through fellowship or association with other Christians. *"Think of ways to encourage one another to outbursts of love and good deeds. And let us not neglect our meeting together, as some people do, but encourage and warn each other, especially now that the day of his coming back again is drawing near"* (Hebrews 10:24-25). We all know that if you take a single coal out of a group of burning coals in a fire it will get cold and die. It is the same with new Christians, they need to be nurtured and encouraged by being around others like them.

As part of a large church that continues to grow, we can easily feel lost in the crowd. So where should we start? The most important place to begin is in the Small Group setting. A Small Group is where we can encounter real friendship, openness and honesty. Here we experience Jesus and grow as new believers, with other group members, by learning to love and care for each other. Without that openness there can be no real community.

---

*Why bother becoming a
part of a small group?*
Acts 2:46-47

Jesus can use other Christians to meet your needs, and he will help others through you, to meet theirs. "We love each other as a result of his loving us first" (1 John 4:19). Jesus gives each one of us gifts. And as we open ourselves up to serve God, the Holy Spirit will enable us to use them   (1 Corinthians 12:4-11). Small Groups are places to have fun and build real supportive friendships and share our spiritual gifts with each other.

The Small Group you attend is a place to see the love of God in action, and come face to face with Jesus. At church there are many Small Groups suitable for all tastes, some of these include: college; couples; singles; mixed; sports; study and recovery groups.

Telling others

One effect of becoming a new believer will be our desire to tell others about the decision we have made. This is developed through prayer, reading the Bible, and meeting with other believers. As a result of receiving so much we'll want to start giving out to others. The way to do this is by being a witness for Jesus, and telling others about the wonderful new life he has given us. Jesus said, *"Go into all the world and preach the Good News to everyone, everywhere"* (Mark 16:15).

We are called to be salt and light in the world, so that those around us will know we are Christians by watching our lives. The key to being a good witness arises out of our relationships with others. There are two dangers that we should be aware of: being insensitive; and being fearful. We have learned about the power of the Holy Spirit and know that He gives us the dynamite power we need to be a witness for Jesus.

---

*How can we be light
and salt to our
neighbors?*
Matthew 5:13-17

As God's representatives we need to be aware that people are very precious to Him. Accordingly, we are responsible to share the good news that Jesus loves them, and died for them, so they too can receive forgiveness of sins and eternal life. With such an awesome responsibility we might pray for boldness.

The apostle Paul said, *"For I am not ashamed of this Good News about Christ. It is the power of God at work, saving everyone who believes"* (Romans 1:16). Therefore, pray to have boldness to share the love of God with others.

Ask that God would open the eyes of unbelievers. The Bible says, *"Satan, the god of this evil world, has blinded the minds of those who don't believe, so they are unable to see the glorious light of the Good News that is shining upon them. They don't understand the message we preach about the glory of Christ, who is the exact likeness of God"* (2 Corinthians 4:4). Now we have received power, we are living examples, able to explain to others how they too can receive a new life in Jesus.

Recommended reading:

The Life You've Always Wanted
John Ortberg, Zondervan

Big Questions

God's Plan for Us

As new Christians, it is important to know God. Jesus wants to guide us and speak to us. To know God's plan for our lives we have to hear his voice. He will usually speak to us in the spiritual realm so it is important to listen with our spiritual ears. Jesus said that his 'sheep' hear his voice (John 10:4).

Remember that Satan will often try and deceive us into thinking we are hearing God's voice when it is really a counterfeit. Due to this we must test all voices with God's lie detector – the Bible.

There are five basic ways to know God's will:

1. The Bible
God's will never contradicts his Word (2 Timothy 2:15). Remember to read the Bible in context, and refer to it in times of decision.

2. The Peace of God
"And let the peace that comes from Christ rule in your hearts. For as members of one body you are all called to live in peace. And always be thankful" (Colossians 3:15). God will give you peace when you make the right decision, based on his Word.

3. Circumstances
Outward things will fall into place as God leads you, primarily from the Bible. *"The Lord says, 'I will guide you along the best pathway for your life. I will advise you and watch over you"* (Psalm 32:8).

4. Ask a mature Christian
Ask for wisdom from a mature Christian in the area you need guidance and discernment. *"For wisdom is better than jewels; and all desirable things cannot compare with her"* (Proverbs 8:11-13).

5. Prayer
God will give us greater spiritual understanding through prayer. *"Don't worry about anything; instead,*

pray about   everything. Tell God what you need, and thank him for all he has done" (Philippians 4: 6).

God's Promises

Once we have made a decision to follow Jesus Christ, God promises to give us strength to follow through with our   commitment. *"For I can do everything with the help of Christ who gives me the strength I need"* (Philippians 4:13). Without Christ we are powerless to overcome sin. We are also promised that whoever remains in Him will not sin. *"So if we continue to live in him, we won't sin either. But those who keep on sinning have never known him or understood who he is"* (1 John 3:6). So now we have a choice, to remain in Him or to choose   otherwise…to sin or not to sin. We are accountable to God for our actions whether they are seen by others or only   ourselves. We are responsible now that we understand the truth about light and darkness, good and evil.

We are encouraged to stick like glue to Jesus. He wants to be our closest friend.

---

*Is Jesus a prophet, a
good man, or
the Son of God?*
Matthew16:13-17

Jesus said, *"But if you stay joined to me and my words remain in you, you may ask any request you like, and it will be granted!"*

31

(John 15:7). What a fabulous promise! This means we no longer have to keep on searching for fulfillment in life, as we now have a permanent position in him. The Bible tells us, "But there is a friend that sticks closer than a brother" (Proverbs 18:24).

God's Church

There are numerous popular misconceptions concerning the church. Many think of it as the building, the pastoral staff, the services, or as a particular denomination. The church is actually made up of the people of God – people like us. *"For you are a chosen people. You are a kingdom of priests, God's holy nation, His very own possession. This is so you can show others the goodness of God, for He called you out of the darkness into His wonderful light"* (1 Peter 2:9).

The universal church (or body of Christians worldwide), consists of approximately 2.2 billion people. This is made up of different denominations; those who are persecuted for their faith; those who are free; those in the third world; and local churches. Within any functioning family there is diversity, unity and mutual dependence.

The church represents people committing to each other and to God, to journey together in faith, accountability and   relationship. Local churches enjoy celebration and special   festive services. These meetings give us a sense of God's   greatness, however, it is difficult to make friends in such a large group. At the weekend service(s) we are able to   recognize many church members, these groups of people are known as congregations.

The congregation is divided into Small Groups. Here we make close friends where confidentiality and accountability take place. *"Always keep yourselves united in the Holy Spirit, and bind yourselves together with peace. We're all one body, we have the same Spirit, and we have all been called to the same glorious future. There is only one Lord, one faith, one baptism, and there is only one God and Father, who is over us all and in us all and living through us all"* (Ephesians 4:3-6). As a believer: God is our Father, Jesus is our brother, and the Holy Spirit is our power to live effective Christian lives - as members of God's family.

Recommended reading:

The Purpose Driven Life by Rick Warren
Zondervan Publishing Company.

Your Pledge

What follows is a personal agreement between you, as a new believer, and the Lord of your life, Jesus. If you want to make this agreement with Him, simply read it through and sign it.

My Personal Agreement

As a new believer and disciple of Jesus, I am making the commitment to follow Him for the rest of my life. I know that Jesus has brought me into a right relationship with my heavenly Father, through His sacrifice on the cross for me. I declare Him to be Lord over my life.

I choose to allow God to transform me into a new person by changing the way I think through reading His Word, the Bible. I will learn how to pray and endeavor to hear and understand God speaking to me. I will commit myself to a Small Group, not only to receive from it, but also to care for others around me. I invite the Holy Spirit to fill my life.

I understand that I am called to obey the commands of Jesus. I am called to love God; love one another; and love those who do not know Him. I am pledging to break with the past, and choose to allow Him to change me daily as I spend time in his presence.

Name: _____

Date: _____

Suggested Prayer

Dear Lord Jesus,

I am sorry for the things I have done wrong in my life. I confess them to You and ask for Your forgiveness.

Thank You that You died on the cross for my sins so that I can be forgiven and set free. I believe that You are the Son of God and that You rose from the dead and are alive today. I ask You to be my Savior and Lord.

Thank You for forgiving me and for the gift of eternal life. Please come into my heart by Your Holy Spirit and be with me forever.

In Jesus' name I pray,

Amen.

www.ingramcontent.com/pod-product-compliance
Lightning Source LLC
Chambersburg PA
CBHW060645030426
42337CB00018B/3453